D1606728

MAKING MOVIES

Movie Soundtracks and Sound Effects

by Geoffrey M. Horn

GARETH**STEVENS**
GS
PUBLISHING
A Member of the WRC Media Family of Companies

Please visit our Web site at: www.garethstevens.com
For a free color catalog describing Gareth Stevens Publishing's
list of high-quality books and multimedia programs, call
1-800-542-2595 (USA) or 1-800-387-3178 (Canada).
Gareth Stevens Publishing's fax: (414) 332-3567.

Library of Congress Cataloging-in-Publication Data

Horn, Geoffrey M.
    Movie soundtracks and sound effects / by Geoffrey M. Horn.
        p. cm. — (Making movies)
    Includes bibliographical references and index.
    ISBN-10: 0-8368-6839-0 — ISBN-13: 978-0-8368-6839-5 (lib. bdg.)
    1. Motion picture music—History and criticism—Juvenile literature.
    2. Motion pictures—Sound effects—History—Juvenile literature.
    I. Title. II. Series: Horn, Geoffrey M. Making movies.
    ML2075.H67   2007
    791.4302'4—dc22   2006007985

This edition first published in 2007 by
Gareth Stevens Publishing
A Member of the WRC Media Family of Companies
330 West Olive Street, Suite 100
Milwaukee, WI 53212 USA

This edition copyright © 2007 by Gareth Stevens, Inc.

Concept: Sophia Olton-Weber
Managing Editor: Valerie J. Weber
Art direction and design: Tammy West
Picture research: Diane Laska-Swanke

Photo credits: Cover, Lucasfilm Ltd./Photofest; p. 5 © Walt Disney/
courtesy Everett Collection; pp. 6, 10, 22 © Everett Collection; p. 8
Warner Brothers/Photofest; p. 13 © Timothy A. Clary/AFP/Getty Images;
p. 14 © Buena Vista Pictures/courtesy Everett Collection; p. 16 © Steve Grayson/
Getty Images; p. 18 © DreamWorks/Everett Collection; p. 19 © MCA/Everett
Collection; p. 21 Fox/Photofest; p. 24 © Columbia/courtesy Everett Collection;
p. 26 © Warner Brothers/courtesy Everett Collection; p. 27 © Miramax/
courtesy Everett Collection; pp. 28-29 Monopole-Pathé/Photofest

Printed in the United States of America

1 2 3 4 5 6 7 8 10 9 09 08 07 06

Contents

Cover: Like earlier *Star Wars* films, *Episode III — Revenge of the 5th* uses the latest high-tech sound effects to create an exciting movie experience.

Sight and Sound

Movies are a visual medium. They tell a story through images, not just words. But movies are more than just moving pictures. They appeal to the ears along with the eyes.

The Power of Sound

Here's what happens when you watch a movie with the sound turned off. A gun fires, but there's no bang. A rocket launches, but you can't feel the roar. A singer's lips move, but no song comes out. The characters laugh, but you don't hear the joke.

When you watch a scary film, notice how sights and sounds work together. You enter a gloomy forest. Dark clouds gather overhead. A bird shrieks. Branches snap. The music grows tense. A voice screams "Look out!" Suddenly — well, you get the idea.

Is a scene spooky? Funny? Violent? Sad? Whatever the feeling, a good film matches sights with sounds to make the scene come alive.

Frozone's ice crackles as the giant robot chasing him crashes through a building. *The Incredibles* earned two Oscars, including one for sound editing.

5

From "Silents" to "Talkies"

Before 1925, films had no soundtrack. These movies are known as silent films, or "silents." The name is a little misleading. The films may have been silent, but the theaters weren't. In big theaters, an orchestra might play along with the movie. Sometimes actors stood behind the screen, reading from a script and making sound effects. Even the smallest theaters had a piano player. The pianist played tunes that fit the mood of the film.

Around 1925, a company called Vitaphone began working with sound for movies. Vitaphone used a machine to record music and voices on discs. Another machine played back the sound while the

A landmark in sound, *The Jazz Singer* (1927) is rarely seen today. The film starred Al Jolson, a white man, who performed in blackface makeup. The blackface style was popular at the time but is now considered racist.

movie was shown. *The Jazz Singer* was the first hit film to use this system. This 1927 movie starred Al Jolson. The soundtrack let people hear as well as see him sing on screen.

Movies with sound-tracks were known as "talking pictures," or "talkies." In 1928, Walt Disney came out with the first cartoon talkie. Called *Steamboat Willie*, the cartoon starred Mickey Mouse. It carefully blended images, dialogue, music, and sound effects. *Steamboat Willie* used a new method of making movie sound. The soundtrack was printed directly on the film. This sound-on-film method soon became the standard for movies.

Behind the Scenes:
What Is Dolby Sound?

Ray Dolby was a video and sound pioneer. During the 1950s, he helped develop the videotape recorder. In the mid-1960s, he found a way to reduce noise in audio recordings. He called this system Dolby A.

Today, many movie theaters use Dolby Digital 5.1. This system produces "surround sound." Surround sound makes you feel like you're in the center of the action.

Dolby 5.1 streams sound into six separate channels. As you face the movie screen, three of these channels are in front of you — left, center, and right. Two other channels carry sounds that come at you from each side. A sixth track makes very low sounds. For example, in a war movie, the sixth channel might make the rumble of tanks. Some theaters have even more complex systems for the highest quality sound.

Sound Design

Today, sound design is a key part of planning a movie. Sound design has three main elements: music, voices, and noises. In early talkies, everything on the soundtrack had to be recorded at the same time. Today, the music, voices, and noises are recorded separately. The sounds are put together, or mixed, after the film has been shot. The person who combines these sounds is known as the sound mixer.

The noises on the soundtrack are called sound effects. They can be simple, like the creak of a floorboard. Or they can be complicated, like the blast of a bomb. The *Star Wars*, *Jurassic Park*, and *Matrix* films rely on sound effects for much of their power.

All the whooshing, crashing, and other sound effects in *The Matrix Reloaded* were carefully crafted.

Scoring a Film

Dahhh-dum! When you watch *Jaws*, you know what those two notes mean. Maybe all you see is the shimmer of water or a flicker of fin. But when you hear those two notes . . . dahhh-dum . . . you know the great white shark is out for blood.

When composer John Williams first played his shark theme for Steven Spielberg, the director was puzzled. "Is that all there is?" he asked. Played softly on the piano, the two notes don't add up to much. Rising from the low strings of a full orchestra, they can make you shiver with terror.

Famous Film Composers

The music for a film is called the score. The score sets the mood for each scene. For example, when the movie has a chase scene, Williams often writes fast, loud, exciting music. In contrast, the music is often slower, quieter, and more romantic for a love

CELEBRITY SNAPSHOT
John Williams

Born: February 8, 1932, in Floral Park, New York

Film Career: Composer

Academy Awards: For his scores for *Fiddler on the Roof* (1971), *Jaws* (1975), *Star Wars* (1977), *E.T. The Extra-Terrestrial* (1982), and *Schindler's List* (1993)

Other Top Films: *Close Encounters of the Third Kind*; *Superman*; *Raiders of the Lost Ark*

Backstory: Williams is the most honored film composer of the last forty years. The American Film Institute called his music for *Star Wars* the top U.S. movie score ever. In *Star Wars*, Williams gives each main character a different theme. For example, the music always signals when Darth Vader is about to appear.

John Williams leads a movie-scoring session.

scene. Williams writes most of his scores for a full orchestra. His scores for the *Star Wars* series have their roots in classical music.

For many years, Alfred Newman was a top composer in Hollywood. Between 1937 and 1970 — the year he died — he was nominated for more than forty Oscars. He won nine times. Thomas Newman, Alfred's son, is one of today's leading film composers. He writes quirky music, full of strong rhythms. His scores draw on classical, jazz, pop, and world-music styles. You may have heard his music in the movie *Lemony Snicket's A Series of Unfortunate Events*.

Another well-known member of the Newman family is Randy Newman. His background is in pop music. He composed the scores and songs for *Toy Story* and other Pixar films.

Songs on the Soundtrack

Soundtracks draw on many different kinds of music. Jazz, soul, disco, rock, heavy metal, techno, and hip-hop have all been used in movies. Sometimes pop songs are added to a soundtrack that already has a full musical score. For example, Celine Dion sings "My Heart Will Go On" at the end of *Titanic*. James Horner composed the movie's score and the song. He won Oscars for both.

Behind the Scenes:
Soundtrack CDs

Some movie soundtracks rank among the top-selling albums of all time. By 2005, for example, the soundtrack CD for *The Bodyguard* had sold 17 million copies. Whitney Houston starred in the 1992 film. She also sang the number-one single "I Will Always Love You." The song's success helped the movie become a huge hit. Other top sellers include the soundtracks for *Saturday Night Fever* and Prince's *Purple Rain*. Soundtracks to *Titanic*, *Dirty Dancing*, and *The Lion King* also sold more than 10 million copies each.

Some movie sound-tracks feature pop songs that have already come out on records. *The Graduate* was one of the first movies to do this. The 1967 film had folk-rock tunes by Simon and Garfunkel. Director Cameron Crowe put many rock oldies in his movie *Almost Famous*. The film *Garden State* uses newer songs to set the mood. So does the TV series *The O.C.*

Filmmakers use songs for many reasons. A soulful tune can heighten the feeling of love or loss. A song can show us what a character is thinking. It can also signal what happens next. For example, imagine a scene in which crooks are planning to rob a bank. A song with "stupid" in the lyrics tells us their plan will probably fail.

CELEBRITY SNAPSHOT
Randy Newman

Born: November 28, 1943, in Los Angeles, California

Film Career: Composer

Academy Awards: Best song for "If I Didn't Have You" from *Monsters, Inc.* (2001)

Other Top Films: *Toy Story; Toy Story 2; Seabiscuit; Cars*

Backstory: Newman was nominated for sixteen Oscars between 1981 and 2001, when he finally won his first. One of his best movie tunes is "When She Loved Me." Sarah McLachlan sings it on the soundtrack for *Toy Story 2*. In this sad song, Cowgirl Jessie, a toy, tells what it's like to be loved and then ignored.

Randy Newman (left) and John Goodman (right) perform Newman's Oscar-winning song from *Monsters, Inc.*

A hot soundtrack can be good for business. Film-makers hope a soundtrack with top artists will attract big audiences for the film. Record companies push to get their artists on movie soundtracks. The firms hope being part of a hit movie will boost the artists' CD sales.

The soundtrack album from *The Lion King* became a top-selling CD in 1994.

Sound Effects

Nearly all films — even quiet dramas — have sound effects. Some of these are real-life sounds. Others are completely made-up. Many effects combine real-life sounds with made-up sounds.

Foley Artists

Someone who adds real-life sounds to movies is called a Foley artist. The name comes from Jack Foley, a sound-effects pioneer. He found clever ways to solve problems with sound. For example, early sound cameras did a poor job of recording footsteps. Foley was a genius at copying how famous actors walked. He re-created the sounds of diffcrent actors' footsteps. Then he added the sounds to the soundtrack.

Foley artists work in a special area called a Foley stage. They know many tricks to fool the ear. Suppose a movie has a scene in which actors crunch through snow. When a winter scene is

15

CELEBRITY SNAPSHOT
Walter Murch

Born: July 12, 1943, in New York City

Film Career: Sound editor, film editor

Academy Awards: For sound on *Apocalypse Now* (1979), film editing and sound on *The English Patient* (1996)

Other Top Films: *The Godfather* series; *The Conversation*; *Ghost*; *Cold Mountain*

Backstory: Murch worked on *The Conversation* with director Francis Ford Coppola. This moody thriller was one of the first movies to explore the power of sound. Murch has a sharp sense of how sight and sound relate. "You have more freedom with sound than you do with picture," he says. "But the big three things — which are emotion, story, and rhythm — apply to sound just as much as they apply to picture." Murch believes filmmakers are always "looking for something that will underline . . . the emotion. . . . You choose sounds that help people to feel the story of what you're doing."

Director Francis Ford Coppola (*left*) joined other top names in Hollywood to honor Walter Murch (*right*) in 2000.

shot outdoors, real snow doesn't sound crunchy enough. Instead, a Foley artist records the sound of boots crunching through sea salt covered with cornstarch. That sound is then used on the soundtrack. In a movie, the starch-salt mixture sounds more like snow than the real thing!

Getting It Right

Movies based on history present major problems. For example, *The Aviator* deals with the life of Howard Hughes. Hughes was an aircraft pioneer. He flew many types of airplanes. Each plane sounded different, from small fighter planes to giant passenger planes. The sound crew on *The Aviator* spent a week recording old planes at airfields in California. Their work made the film feel real.

Behind the Scenes:
Awards for Sound and Music

Each year, the movie industry hands out Academy Awards for sound editing and sound mixing. The award for sound editing usually goes to the sound designer. In addition, Oscars are given for the best musical score and song. The Golden Globe Awards also honor the year's top score and song.

The recording industry gives out Grammy Awards. Each year, Grammy voters choose the best movie or TV soundtrack album. They also pick the top song written for a movie or TV show.

With terrifying realism, *Saving Private Ryan* captures the sights and sounds of war.

Saving Private Ryan, a movie directed by Steven Spielberg, is a landmark in sound design. The film opens with a key battle of World War II (1939–1945) — the D-day invasion in 1944. The scene shows American soldiers storming a beach in Normandy, France. The sound design places you in the middle of the action. Bullets whiz by your head. Cannon shells explode all around you. Sound artist Gary Rydstrom won two Oscars for his work on the movie.

Creating New Worlds

Rydstrom faced a different challenge on *Jurassic Park*. For this dinosaur movie, Spielberg knew he needed a *Tyrannosaurus rex*. The *T. rex* would make noise when it breathed, growled, or stomped through a forest. But what did a *T. rex* sound like?

Since dinosaurs don't exist anymore, Rydstrom couldn't just go out and record one. Instead, he recorded sounds from whales, elephants, horses, and other animals. He combined bits and pieces of all these sounds for the *T. rex* and other dinosaurs in the movie.

Gary Rydstrom layered snorts, wails, and growls from different animals to create the dinosaur sounds in *Jurassic Park*.

If you've seen the 1977 *Star Wars*, you probably recall the seedy bar where Luke first meets Han Solo. The bar is filled with creatures who sound as weird as they look. Sound designers created different voices and languages for all these creatures.

Ben Burtt designed the voices of R2-D2 and Chewbacca. To make the sound of a lightsaber, he started with the hum of an old movie projector. Next, he recorded the buzz from a TV picture tube. He combined the two sounds and played them through a speaker. Finally he re-recorded the sounds by waving a microphone in front of the speaker. The faster he whipped the mic, the quicker the lightsaber seemed to be moving!

CHAPTER 4

Hollywood and Broadway

Broadway's strength is live theater. Hollywood makes films. Broadway is in New York City. Hollywood is part of Los Angeles. Nearly 3,000 miles (4,800 kilometers) separate the Great White Way from Tinseltown. But they have a closer connection than you might think.

Birth of the Musical

A musical is a play or film with lots of singing and dancing. Recent movie musicals include *Rent* and *Chicago*. Both shows played on Broadway before they were made into films.

Broadway is where the modern musical took shape a century ago. Then as now, people flocked to the Great White Way to see the hottest shows. During the silent era, Hollywood couldn't compete with Broadway. But when talkies were invented, the film studios saw their chance. Movies could bring the magic of Broadway to theaters everywhere.

CELEBRITY SNAPSHOT
Sir Elton John

Born: March 25, 1947, in Pinner, Middlesex, England

Film Career: Composer, singer, actor

Academy Awards: For the song "Can You Feel the Love Tonight" from *The Lion King* (1994)

Other Top Films: *Tommy; The Road to El Dorado*

Backstory: Elton John was a famous pop star long before he became a movie composer. On *The Lion King* and *The Road to El Dorado*, Elton John worked with another Englishman, Tim Rice. Rice wrote the words. John wrote the music. Rice has also worked with another British songwriter, Andrew Lloyd Webber. The two men also wrote *Evita* and *Joseph and the Amazing Technicolor Dreamcoat*.

Elton John was a famous pop star long before he became a movie composer.

The first full-length movie musical appeared in 1929. It was called *The Broadway Melody*.

Dance, Dance, Dance

The 1930s and early 1940s marked a great era for movie musicals. These were tough times for many Americans. First, the economy went into a deep slump. Many people lost their jobs, homes, farms, and businesses. Then, the nation fought in World War II. People wanted happy movies to take their minds off their troubles.

Fred Astaire was a top talent during this period. He starred on Broadway before coming to Hollywood. Astaire was a fabulous dancer. During the 1930s, he and Ginger Rogers danced together in nine films. Her skilled moves and sassy spirit made her a perfect partner.

Ginger Rogers and Fred Astaire kick up their heels in *Swing Time*.

Another big name in Hollywood musicals was Busby Berkeley. He became famous as a dance director, although he had no dance training. His dance numbers featured hundreds of beautiful women in dazzling costumes. He used wonderful sets, amazing special effects, and creative camera angles. One of his best-known films is *42nd Street*. Like so many Hollywood musicals of this era, it's a story about Broadway!

From Stage to Screen to Stage

Berkeley's career faded after World War II. But Hollywood continued to use Broadway's talents. Many big Broadway shows made it to the big screen. Film versions of *West Side Story* and *My Fair Lady* won Oscars for best picture in the 1960s. So did *The Sound of Music*.

In the mid-1980s, big-screen musicals reached a dead end. They were costly to make. Many of them were duds. Too many of them lost money.

Behind the Scenes:
So You'd Like to Be a Film Composer . . . ?

The best way to learn how to make music is — to make music! Learn how to play an instrument. Join school music groups. Play in a band with your friends. Try out different styles. Start writing your own short pieces. (Computer programs like GarageBand make composing easy and fun.) If you know someone who is shooting a video, offer to write the score.

Nearly all colleges give music courses. The Berklee College of Music is known for its classes in film scoring. The school is in Boston, Massachusetts.

Then, the Disney studio had an idea. Decades earlier, Disney cartoon musicals had been big moneymakers. Would a new cartoon musical with catchy tunes enchant movie fans? The answer was yes. *The Little Mermaid* earned more than $100 million in 1989.

Successes kept coming for Disney in the early 1990s. *Beauty and the Beast* and *The Lion King* were huge, worldwide hits. These two films' scores and songs were as good as anything on Broadway. For many years, Hollywood had borrowed from the Great White Way. Now Broadway returned the compliment. *Beauty and the Beast* and *The Lion King* were turned into stage musicals. They became two of the most successful shows in Broadway history.

Jonathan Larson wrote the lyrics and music for *Rent*, a Broadway musical that reached the big screen in 2005.

Changing with the Times

History was made in 1955 when *The Blackboard Jungle* opened. The film showed the struggle between teachers and young punks in a big-city school. The soundtrack started with a record by Bill Haley and His Comets. The name of that record? "Rock Around the Clock"! The rock 'n' roll era in films had begun.

Tunes and Trends

Hollywood has always changed with the times. When Elvis Presley topped the pop charts, he also was a major movie star. When the Beatles ruled the rock world, movies helped spread their fame. The Beatles made three hit films. Two — *A Hard Day's Night* and *Help!* — were live-action features. Their third movie success was *Yellow Submarine*, a full-length cartoon.

25

CELEBRITY SNAPSHOT

Danny Elfman

Born: May 29, 1953, in Amarillo, Texas

Film Career: Composer, actor

Academy Awards: Nominated for scores to *Good Will Hunting* (1997), *Men in Black* (1997), and *Big Fish* (2003)

Other Top Films: *Beetlejuice; Batman; Spider-Man*

Backstory: Elfman first became known as a member of the band Oingo Boingo. He has composed music for most of Tim Burton's movies. In Burton's *Charlie and the Chocolate Factory*, Elfman was the singing voice of the Oompa-Loompas. You probably know his theme music for *The Simpsons*.

In Charlie and the Chocolate Factory, **Deep Roy acted the Oompa-Loompas, but Danny Elfman sang the songs.**

Rap star Queen Latifah was brassy and sassy as "Mama" in the movie musical *Chicago*.

During the early 1970s, soul stars like Isaac Hayes and Marvin Gaye wrote movie scores. Later, songs from *Saturday Night Fever* became pop-disco hits. In the 1980s, Danny Elfman emerged from the new-wave scene to become a film composer.

Hip-hop has made a big splash on movie screens and soundtracks. Screen stars Will Smith and Queen Latifah got their start in rap and hip-hop. So did Ice Cube, LL Cool J, and DMX. Eminem's hip-hop musical *8 Mile* struck a chord with critics and audiences. His smash single "Lose Yourself" won the Oscar for best song of 2002.

Behind the Scenes:
Welcome to Bollywood

Each year, India turns out more than eight hundred movies. Most of these films are filled with romance, drama — and music. Featuring exciting songs and dances, they usually last about three hours.

India's film industry was born in Bombay. (Today, the city is called Mumbai.) Filmmakers thought of Bombay as the Hollywood of India. That's how the name "Bollywood" got started.

A well-known Bollywood musical is *Devdas*. It is in the Hindi language. Aishwarya Rai has a big role in the film. She is one of India's top stars. She also appears in the English-language *Bride & Prejudice*.

Today's films draw on the music of many lands. Scores by Philip Glass use instruments from many different sources. Filmmakers from India, China, and other countries use the sounds of their homelands in their movies.

The thrilling song-and-dance numbers in *Devdas* helped make this Bollywood musical a worldwide sensation.

The Digital Age

Sound recording has come a long way in one hundred years. Early records sound tinny and scratchy. Today's soundtracks sparkle with world-class digital sound.

Movie theater sound has improved greatly since the 1970s. George Lucas deserves much of the credit. Creator of the *Star Wars* movies, he also founded Skywalker Sound. Famous sound designers such as Ben Burtt and Randy Thom work for Skywalker. The company creates sound effects for twenty to thirty films each year.

Thanks to the invention of the DVD, you can enjoy great sound at home. DVDs can play in

stereo over headphones or computer speakers. Or they can provide surround sound in a home-theater setup.

Recent DVDs include many listening options. For example, *Star Wars III — Revenge of the Sith* lets you listen to the dialogue in English, French, or Spanish. You can also hear comments by George Lucas and others who worked on the movie. The DVD allows you to hear the music and sound effects with startling clarity. It also shows you how the movie-makers matched sights with sounds to harness the full power of film.

Glossary

abrupt — sudden.

Academy Award — also called an Oscar; an award given out by the movie industry.

backstory — the background story to something seen on screen.

dialogue — in a screenplay, the words the characters say to each other.

digital — created by computer.

director — the person who controls the creative part of making a movie.

Foley artist — someone who re-creates real-life sounds for movies.

musical — a film or play with lots of singing and dancing.

nominated — named or suggested as a candidate for a particular honor or position.

orchestra — a group of people playing a variety of musical instruments.

score — the music composed for a movie or play.

sound design — an overall plan for how a movie will use music, voices, and noises.

soundtrack — the part of the movie film on which sound is recorded, including the dialogue, music, and sound effects.

talkies — short for "talking pictures"; movies with a soundtrack.

To Find Out More

Books

100 Careers in the Music Business. Tanja L. Crouch
(Barron's Educational Series)

Ten Great American Composers. Collective Biographies
(series). Carmen Bredeson and Ralph Thibodeau
(Enslow)

Videos

Jurassic Park (MCA Home Video) PG-13

The Lion King (Walt Disney Video) G

That's Entertainment! The Complete Collection
(Warner Home Video) G

Yellow Submarine (MGM) G

Web Sites

Howstuffworks: "How Movie Sound Works"
entertainment.howstuffworks.com/movie-sound1.htm
Different movie sound systems explained

Film Sound Design
www.filmsound.org
Articles, interviews, and discussions of film sound

Publisher's note to educators and parents: Our editors have carefully reviewed
these Web sites to ensure that they are suitable for children. Many Web sites change
frequently, however, and we cannot guarantee that a site's future contents will
continue to meet our high standards of quality and educational value. Be advised
that children should be closely supervised whenever they access the Internet.

Index

About the Author

Geoffrey M. Horn has been a fan of music, movies, and sports for as long as he can remember. He has written more than three dozen books for young people and adults, along with hundreds of articles for encyclopedias and other works. He lives in southwestern Virginia, in the foothills of the Blue Ridge Mountains, with his wife, their collie, and four cats. He dedicates this book to the memory of Rose Laderman and Estelle Strauss.